Place Value & Number Sense

2nd Grade Math Workbook Series Vol 1

Speedy Publishing LLC
40 E. Main St. #1156
Newark, DE 19711
www.speedypublishing.com

Write the number in expanded form.

	hundreds	tens	ones
483	400	80	3
599			
674			

	hundreds	tens	ones
839			
859			
106			
626			

	hundreds	tens	ones
597			
96			
488			
479			

	hundreds	tens	ones
554			
896			
893			
83			

	hundreds	tens	ones
772			
879			
191			
188			

	hundreds	tens	ones
377			
479			
139			
391			

	hundreds	tens	ones
200			
88			
521			
463			

	hundreds	tens	ones
548			
476			
649			
270			

	hundreds	tens	ones
715			
639			
521			
202			

	hundreds	tens	ones
578			
454			
243			
402			

	hundreds	tens	ones
257			
130			
796			
99			

	hundreds	tens	ones
360			
178			
274			
353			

	hundreds	tens	ones
553			
375			
482			
745			

	hundreds	tens	ones
358			
762			
576			
548			

	hundreds	tens	ones
542			
755			
671			
587			

	hundreds	tens	ones
183			
481			
728			
861			

	hundreds	tens	ones
752			
426			
278			
264			

	hundreds	tens	ones
231			
559			
401			
661			

	hundreds	tens	ones
141			
547			
795			
412			

Arrange the numbers from largest to smallest.

1	698	843	563
	______	______	______
2	130	251	559
	______	______	______
3	979	511	574
	______	______	______
4	776	931	299
	______	______	______

5	177	437	962
	______	______	______
6	378	241	504
	______	______	______
7	248	725	231
	______	______	______
8	497	306	606
	______	______	______
9	242	117	173
	______	______	______

10	305	955	928
	______	______	______
11	907	509	615
	______	______	______
12	228	796	899
	______	______	______
13	960	868	452
	______	______	______
14	169	570	351
	______	______	______

15 547 322 272

16 218 752 846

17 563 599 917

18 987 243 478

19 825 190 685

20	378	258	474
	______	______	______
21	371	310	442
	______	______	______
22	819	904	830
	______	______	______
23	639	587	755
	______	______	______
24	209	282	846
	______	______	______

Find the missing place value from a 3-digit number

1. 300 + ________ + 5 = 385

2. 3 + 40 + ________ = 243

3. ________ + 400 + 80 = 481

4. __________ + 10 + 300 = 317

5. __________ + 3 + 200 = 253

6. 30 + 1 + __________ = 631

7. 6 + __________ + 900 = 976

8. 2 + 20 + __________ = 522

9. __________ + 90 + 800 = 893

10. __________ + 70 + 3 = 573

11. 7 + 400 + __________ = 427

12. 5 + 90 + __________ = 895

13. 10 + __________ + 500 = 519

14. 8 + __________ + 400 = 438

15. 600 + 50 + __________ = 659

16. 50 + 7 + ______ = 157

17. __________ + 30 + 7 = 837

18. 1 + __________ + 70 = 871

19. 0 + 30 + __________ = 230

20. 4 + ________ + 600 = 674

21. 4 + ________ + 400 = 444

22. 2 + ________ + 200 = 232

23. ________ + 70 + 800 = 875

24. 40 + __________ + 100 = 142

25. 400 + 60 + __________ = 468

Build a three-digit number from the parts

1. 6 + 40 + 300 = ________

2. 1 + 50 + 600 = ________

3. 3 + 0 + 900 = ________

4. 300 + 80 + 4 = ________

5. 1 + 60 + 200 = ________

6. 500 + 40 + 9 = ________

7. 70 + 4 + 300 = ________

8. 70 + 2 + 500 = ________

9. 9 + 500 + 80 = ________

10. 9 + 70 + 500 = ________

11. 70 + 1 + 400 = ________

12. 8 + 400 + 40 = ________

13. 9 + 90 + 700 = ________

14. 8 + 60 + 600 = ________

15. 2 + 500 + 60 = ________

ANSWERS

	H	T	O
483	400	80	3
599	500	90	9
674	600	70	4
839	800	30	9
859	800	5	9
106	100	0	6
626	600	20	6
597	500	90	7
96		90	6
488	400	80	8
479	400	70	9
554	500	50	4
896	800	90	6
893	800	90	3
83	0	80	3

	H	T	O
772	700	70	2
879	800	70	9
191	100	90	1
188	100	80	8
377	300	70	7
479	400	70	9
139	100	30	9
391	300	90	1
200	0	200	0
88	0	80	8
521	500	20	1
463	400	60	3
548	500	40	8
476	400	70	6
649	600	40	9

	H	T	O
270	200	70	0
715	700	10	5
639	600	30	9
521	500	20	1
202	200	0	2
578	500	70	8
454	400	50	4
243	200	40	3
402	400	0	2
257	200	50	7
130	100	30	0
796	700	90	6
99	0	90	9
360	300	60	0
178	100	70	8

	H	T	O
274	200	70	4
353	300	50	3
553	500	50	3
375	300	70	5
482	400	80	2
745	700	40	5
358	300	50	8
762	700	60	2
576	500	70	6
548	500	40	8

	H	T	O
542	500	40	2
755	700	50	5
671	600	70	1
587	500	80	7
183	100	80	3
481	400	80	1
728	700	20	8
861	800	60	1
752	700	50	2
426	400	20	6

	H	T	O
278	200	70	8
264	200	60	4
231	200	30	1
559	500	50	9
401	400	0	1
661	600	60	1
141	100	40	1
547	500	40	7
795	700	90	5
412	400	10	2

1	843	698	563
2	559	251	130
3	979	574	511
4	931	776	299
5	962	437	177
6	504	378	241
7	725	248	231
8	606	497	306
9	242	173	117
10	955	928	305
11	907	615	509
12	899	796	228
13	960	868	452
14	570	351	169
15	547	322	272
16	846	752	218
17	917	599	563
18	987	478	243
19	825	685	190
20	474	378	258
21	442	371	310
22	904	830	819
23	755	639	587
24	846	282	209

1. 80
2. 200
3. 1
4. 7
5. 50
6. 600
7. 70
8. 500
9. 3
10. 500
11. 20
12. 800
13. 9
14. 30
15. 9
16. 100
17. 800
18. 800
19. 200
20. 70
21. 40
22. 30
23. 5
24. 2
25. 8

1. 346
2. 651
3. 903
4. 384
5. 261
6. 549
7. 374
8. 572
9. 589
10. 579
11. 471
12. 448
13. 799
14. 668
15. 562

www.ingramcontent.com/pod-product-compliance
Lightning Source LLC
LaVergne TN
LVHW082307150826
845677LV00009B/1739